SUMMER BRIDGE LEARNING FOR
MINECRAFTERS
Bridging Grades K-1

by Nancy Rogers Bosse
Illustrated by Amanda Brack

SKY PONY PRESS

Copyright © 2018 by Hollan Publishing, Inc.

Minecraft® is a registered trademark of Notch Development AB.

The Minecraft game is copyright © Mojang AB.

Sky Pony Press books may be purchased in bulk at special discounts for sales promotion, corporate gifts, fund-raising, or educational purposes. Special editions can also be created to specifications. For details, contact the Special Sales Department, Sky Pony Press, 307 West 36th Street, 11th Floor, New York, NY 10018 or info@skyhorsepublishing.com.

Sky Pony® is a registered trademark of Skyhorse Publishing, Inc.®, a Delaware corporation.

Minecraft® is a registered trademark of Notch Development AB.
The Minecraft game is copyright © Mojang AB.

Visit our website at www.skyponypress.com.

Authors, books, and more at SkyPonyPressBlog.com.

10 9 8 7 6 5 4 3 2 1

Library of Congress Cataloging-in-Publication Data is available on file.

Cover design by Brian Peterson
Cover illustration by Bill Greenhead

Interior design by Kevin Baier

Interior illustrations by Amanda Brack
All other art used by permission from Shutterstock.com

Print ISBN: 978-1-5107-3596-5

Printed in China

SUMMER BRIDGE LEARNING FOR

MINECRAFTERS

Bridging Grades K-1

by Nancy Rogers Bosse
Illustrated by Amanda Brack

Sky Pony Press
New York

A NOTE TO PARENTS

You probably know the importance of having your child practice the key skills taught in the classroom. And you are probably hoping that your kid will be on board with practicing at home. Well, congratulations! You've come to the right place! *Summer Bridge for Minecrafters, Bridging Grades K–1* transforms learning into an adventure complete with zombies, skeletons, and creepers.

You will love that *Summer Bridge for Minecrafters, Bridging Grades K–1* aligns with the National Core Standards for math and English language arts (ELA), as well as national, state, and district recommendations for science and social studies. Every page reinforces a key concept in one of the subject areas. Your child will love the colorful art, familiar video game characters, and the fun approach to each learning activity!

The pages of this workbook are color coded to help you target specific skills areas as needed.

BLUE	**Language Arts**
ORANGE	**Math**
GREEN	**Science**
PINK	**Social Studies**

Whether it's the joy of seeing their favorite Minecraft characters on every page, the fun of solving a riddle or a puzzle, or the pride of accomplishment of completing a page, there is something in this book for even the most reluctant learner.

Happy adventuring!

CONTENTS

WRITING LETTERS

Trace the letters.

Aa

Bb Cc Dd Ee

Ff Gg Hh Ii

Jj Kk Ll Mm

MORE LETTERS

Trace the letters.

> ## JUST FOR FUN
>
> **Question:** Why are zombies so good at destroying?
>
> **Answer:** They have dead-ication.

N n

O o   P p   Q q   R r

S s   T t   U u   V v

W w   X x   Y y   Z z

BEGINNING SOUNDS

Trace the letter. Then circle at least one item that starts with the letter. Hint: There may be more than one.

1.

2.

3.

4.

5.

BEGINNING SOUNDS

Trace the letter. Then circle at least one item that starts with the letter.

1. C c

2. F f

3. M m

4. R r

5. W w

RHYMING WORDS

Draw a line to connect the rhyming words.

Jeepers Creepers! We love to rhyme.

1.

Cat

2.

Egg

3.

Clock

4.

Porch

5.

Head

A.

B.

C.

D.

E.

LONG OR SHORT VOWEL SOUND

*Say each word. Listen for the vowel sound.
Circle long or short.*

1. Witch

long   short

2. Creeper

long   short

3. Cat

long   short

4. Squid

long   short

5. Axe

long   short

6. Race

long   short

7. Ghast

long   short

8. Bed

long   short

9. Mule

long   short

SHORT VOWELS

Draw a line to connect the word with the short vowel sound to the matching picture.

1. pig

A.

2. cat

B.

3. bed

C.

4. ocelot

D.

5. sun

E.

SHORT VOWELS

Circle the word with the short vowel sound that matches each picture.

1.

cap

lap

map

2.

egg

tag

pig

3.

dish

fish

wish

4.

back

block

black

5.

web

wet

wag

6.

bat

hat

rat

7.

rug

bug

hug

8.

squid

sit

sad

The silent *e* at the end of the word makes the vowel long.

LONG VOWELS

All the words below have long vowel sounds. Write the missing vowel in each word.

1. c __ k e

2. b __ n e

3. m __ l e

4. r __ d e

5. c __ b e

LONG VOWELS

The first vowel in each word below is long. Draw a line to connect the word to the matching picture.

1. tree

A.

2. boat

B.

3. wheat

C.

4. suit

D.

5. rain

E.

ASK AND ANSWER QUESTIONS

Read the story. Answer the questions.

THE LIBRARY

The library is filled with books about building. Mobs come to the library to find a book of enchantment. Today Steve is going to the library. He wants to find a special book to make him more powerful so he can defeat the Wither.

Once inside the library, Steve meets the librarian. The librarian tells him he must climb the stairs and find the trap door. Then he will find the book.

It is dark in the library. Steve must carry a torch. Finally, Steve finds his way to the trap door. He pulls a lever. The door opens. Inside the room, he finds the book he was looking for. He takes the book home and learns how to enchant his weapons. Later that day, he defeats the Wither!

1. Where did Steve go?

2. Why did he go there?

3. Did Steve defeat the Wither?

PARTS OF A STORY

The setting is where the story happens. The plot is what happens in the story.

*Read the story. Draw a picture that shows the **setting** and **plot** of the story.*

CREEPER TROUBLE

The creeper waits behind a tree in the Forest Biome. There is a ledge nearby. The creeper wants to destroy anything that comes near.

A player comes around the corner. The creeper jumps out. "sssSSS-Say there," the creeper says. "sssSSSSorry you have to go sssSSS-SosssSSSSoon." It explodes and knocks the player off the ledge! Goodbye, player!

STRUCTURE OF A STORY

Read or listen to the story. Draw pictures to tell the story.

STEVE MEETS A ZOMBIE

It is late. The sun has already gone down. Steve walks through the woods.

Suddenly, a zombie attacks! They battle. Steve shoots his bow and arrow. The zombie hits back hard. Steve shoots another arrow, but the zombie fights back. Steve shoots one final arrow.

Zing! Steve destroys the zombie.

beginning

middle

ending

STRUCTURE OF A STORY

Read or listen to the story. Draw pictures to tell the story.

beginning

middle

ending

SKELETON ATTACK!

"The skeletons are coming," Steve shouted. A group of skeletons followed right behind Steve as he ran back to his farm to protect it. His loyal dog was right beside him.

Steve turned around and drew his golden sword. He struck one skeleton while his dog leaped up to bite the other skeletons. The skeletons were no match for this team. Two of the bony beasts were destroyed. The rest ran away.

Steve gathered the bones and arrows with a big smile. The farm was saved!

WORDS AND PICTURES

Read or listen to this informational text about the city. Look at the picture. Then answer the questions on the next page.

THE CITY

A very experienced gamer built this block city. It is made of blocks of clay and glass.

The city has tall buildings. There is a church, a school, shops, and many houses.

Some villagers live in the city. They have many jobs. Visiting villagers come to the city for a vacation. There are many ways to get around the city. Villagers can walk, ride the train, or take a boat.

Answer the questions about the city. Circle W if you get the answer from the words. Circle P if you get the answer from the picture. Circle both if you used both the words and picture to answer the question.

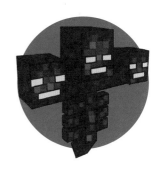

1. What is the city near?   W   P

_____

_____

2. What is the city made of?   W   P

_____

_____

3. What does the city look like?   W   P

_____

_____

_____

_____

4. Who is in the city?   W   P

_____

_____

5. How can villagers get around the city?   W   P

_____

_____

_____

WHAT DOES IT MEAN?

*Read each sentence. Use the context to figure out the meaning of the **bolded** word. Then circle the best meaning.*

1. The **hostile** mobs are not friendly.

    HOSTILE means:

        nice   *or*   mean

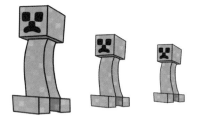

2. The **residents** live in the city.

    RESIDENTS are:

        people who live in a place   *or*   monsters who destroy

3. The mobs **spawn** baby mobs.

    SPAWN means:

        to destroy   *or*   to create

4. The Minecraft **biomes** include Jungle, Ice Plains, Forest, and the End.

    BIOMES are:

        mobs   *or*   places

WHAT DOES IT MEAN?

*Read each sentence. Use the context to figure out the meaning of the **bolded** word. Then circle the best meaning.*

1. The **neutral** mobs will not help or hurt you.

   NEUTRAL means:

   neither bad nor good   **or**   angry and attacking

2. Sheep and rabbits live in the large trees of the **taiga**.

   TAIGA means:

   a hot desert   **or**   a swampy forest

3. The **void** is pure black and empty.

   VOID means:

   nothing there   **or**   full of life

4. The creeper's explosions make it a **destructive** mob.

   DESTRUCTIVE means:

   friendly   **or**   dangerous

FIND THE DIFFERENCE

Cross out the picture that is different.

1.

2.

3.

4.

5.

FIND THE DIFFERENCE

Cross out the picture that is different.

Look!
We're different.

1.

2.

3.

4.

5.

23

OPPOSITES

Draw a line to each opposite

1.  sit

2.  little

3. day

4. friendly

A. night

B. hostile

C. big

D. stand

CATEGORIES

Label each category.

red	green	2 legs	4 legs	living	non living

1.

_____

2.

_____

3.

_____

4.

_____

5.

_____

6.

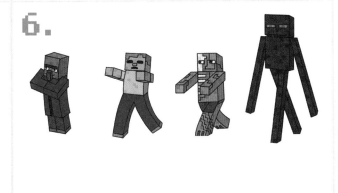

_____

25

CATEGORIES

Draw each item in the correct category.

ANIMAL	FOOD

WEAPON	PLANTS

POSITION WORDS

Look at the picture. Circle the word that best completes each sentence.

1. Ocelot is   **by**   **behind**   the river.

2. Monkey sits   **on**   **under**   the tree.

3. The clouds float   **under**   **in**   the sky.

4. Parrot flies   **below**   **above**   the river.

5. The trees grow   **inside**   **beside**   the river.

A noun is a person, place, or thing.

NOUNS

Find and circle the nouns listed at the bottom of the page.

ball	book	lamp	shoe
bear	doll	pillow	sock
bed	duck	plant	truck

PLURALS

Write the plural.

Plural means more than one. Most nouns are made plural by adding *s*.

To make the plural of words that end in o, s, x, ch, sh, or th, add *es*.

Example: *one boss   two boss**es***

 1. pig _____

 2. potato _____

 3. witch _____

 4. cow _____

 5. bush _____

Verbs are action words. 'Hang' is a verb.

VERBS

Write the verb that matches the picture.

| run | fight | swim | eat | fly |
| think | ride | laugh | sit |

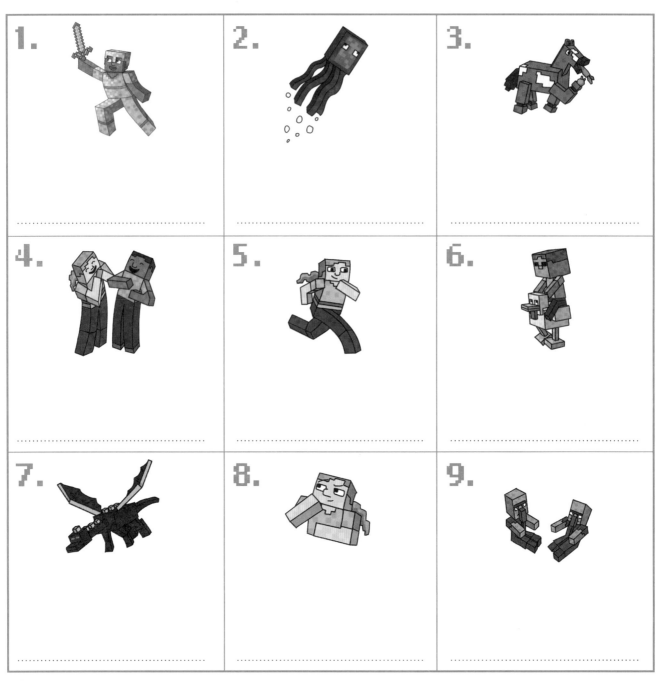

1.

....

2.

....

3.

....

4.

....

5.

....

6.

....

7.

....

8.

....

9.

....

PAST TENSE

Draw a line from the present tense verb to its irregular past tense form.

Past tense shows something already happened.

Most verbs show past tense by adding *ed*. Not these words!

1. run

2. fight

3. eat

4. ride

5. think

A. rode

B. fought

C. thought

D. ran

E. ate

FIX THE SENTENCE

Copy the sentence. Fix the errors.

1. the snow golem is a mob

_____

2. it has two snow blocks and a pumpkin head

_____

3. it throws snowballs

_____

4. does it melt when it gets hot

_____

5. does it melt in the rain

_____

END PUNCTUATION

Place the correct punctuation at the end of each sentence.

Most sentences end with . Exciting sentences end with ! Questions end with ?

1. The creeper is about to explode

2. Steve made a new sword

3. Where is the snow golem

4. What time is it

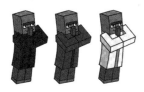

5. The villagers have many jobs

6. The map shows the way home

7. The witch is about to throw her potion

8. Steve can run fast

33

WRITING SENTENCES

Rearrange the words to write a sentence. Don't forget to start with a capital letter and end with a period.

1.    the   cuts   Steve   cake

   _____

2.   dragon   through   flies   blocks

   _____

3.   Overworld   in   grow   trees   the

   _____

4.    pigs   Alex   and   cares   chickens   for

   _____

WRITING SENTENCES

Write sentences about the picture. Use words from the word box.

playground	swing	rings	chalk
play	boy	girl	basketball

1. _____

2. _____

3. _____

4. _____

A fact is something that can be proven to be true.

FACT OR OPINION

Write a fact about each mob.

1. **Example:**

The pig is pink.

2.  Steve is ....

3. The potion is ....

4.  The spider is ....

IN MY OPINION

A mob is a video game character. Which one is the best one, in your opinion? Write your opinion below and then draw a picture of the mob.

I am the best-looking mob.

That's your opinion.

In my opinion, _____ is the best mob

because _____ .

THE BEST MOB

WRITE A STORY

Use the characters and setting pictured to write a short Minecrafting story. Say the story out loud and have someone help you write it, or try to write it yourself!

CHARACTERS

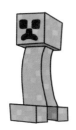

creeper

zombie

Alex

SETTING

Jungle Biome

_____

_____

_____

_____

_____

_____

_____

WRITE A STORY

Use the characters and setting pictured to write a short Minecrafting story. Say the story out loud and have someone help you write it, or try to write it yourself!

CHARACTERS

snow golem

bunny

Steve

SETTING

Arctic Biome

SEQUENCE EVENTS

Read the passage. Then number the steps (1, 2, 3, 4) to show how to mine for diamonds.

Mining Diamonds

It's easy and fun to mine for diamonds. First, you need to locate a block of diamond ore. Ore is rock that has diamonds in it. Then, chop the diamond ore with an iron pickaxe. When a diamond drops, place it in a chest for safe keeping. Then you can use it to make a diamond sword!

Use the diamond to make a sword.

Put the diamond in the chest.

Locate a block of diamond ore.

Use an iron pickaxe to break the block.

SEQUENCE EVENTS

Read the passage. Then number the pictures (1, 2, 3, 4) to show how to ride a pig.

How to Ride a Pig

If you're an advanced Minecrafter, you can learn to ride a pig! First, get all the things you need. You need a pig, a saddle, a carrot, and a stick. Next, put the saddle on the pig's back. Then, hook the carrot onto the end of the stick and hold it in front of the pig. Now jump on the pig and enjoy the ride!

Put the saddle on the pig.

 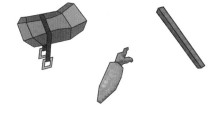

You will need a pig, a saddle, a carrot, and a stick.

Jump on the pig.

Hook the carrot on the stick and hold it out.

ADDING DETAILS

Rewrite the sentence, adding adjectives and adverbs to make the sentence more interesting.

Adjectives (describe people and things)			Adverbs (describe actions)		
creepy	huge		slowly	creepily	
dangerous	grumpy	green	quietly	quickly	sneakily

1. The _____ squid swam _____.

....

....

2. The _____ witch _____ made a potion.

....

....

3. The _____ spider crawled _____.

....

....

4. The _____ dragon flew _____.

....

....

ADDING DETAILS

Sentences are made of nouns, verbs, and prepositional phrases. Use the words from each row of the word box to answer the questions. Then, write a complete sentence.

Nouns	Verbs	Prepositional Phrases
1. creeper	exploded	in the village
2. zombie	attacked	in a cave
3. skeleton	spawned	in a pit

1. What? ....

Did what? ....

Where? ....

....

....

2. What? ....

Did what? ....

Where? ....

....

....

3. What? ....

Did what? ....

Where? ....

....

....

IT'S IN THE DETAILS

Draw a picture to tell a story. Include lots of details in your picture.

The Terrible Night

IT'S IN THE DETAILS

Draw a picture to tell a story. Include lots of details in your picture.

On the Farm

NUMBERS 0 TO 9

Use the chart to color the numbers and identify two dangerous mobs.

1 – black   4 – light pink   7 – light green
2 – medium green   5 – gray   8 – medium pink
3 – dark green   6 – dark gray   9 – white

7	3	2	7	3	2	3	7
3	1	1	3	2	1	1	3
2	1	1	2	3	1	1	2
3	2	3	1	1	3	2	3
7	3	2	1	1	2	3	7
2	1	1	1	1	1	1	2
3	1	2	7	3	2	1	3
7	2	7	3	2	7	3	2

5	5	3	3	4	8	4	4
5	5	5	3	4	4	8	4
5	1	9	3	4	1	9	4
5	5	3	6	6	4	4	8
5	5	3	6	6	4	4	4
5	5	3	4	4	8	4	4
5	5	3	4	4	4	8	4
5	5	3	3	3	3	3	3

What two dangerous mobs do you see above?

....

....

....

LET'S COUNT

Count. Write the number.

1.

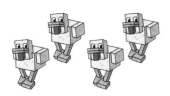

4
_____

2.

_____

3.

_____

4.

_____

5.

_____

6.

_____

7.

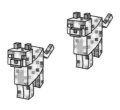

_____

8.

_____

9.

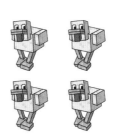

_____

COUNTING ON THE FARM

Look at the picture and answer the questions below.

How many animals? _____

How many legs in all? _____

COUNTING IN THE OCEAN

Count each kind of fish and write the number below.

shark _____   squid _____   crab _____

blue fish _____   orange fish _____

purple fish _____   pink fish _____

COUNTING NUMBERS

Connect the dots to brew some potion. Color the picture light blue to make potion of Swiftness and red for potion of Strength.

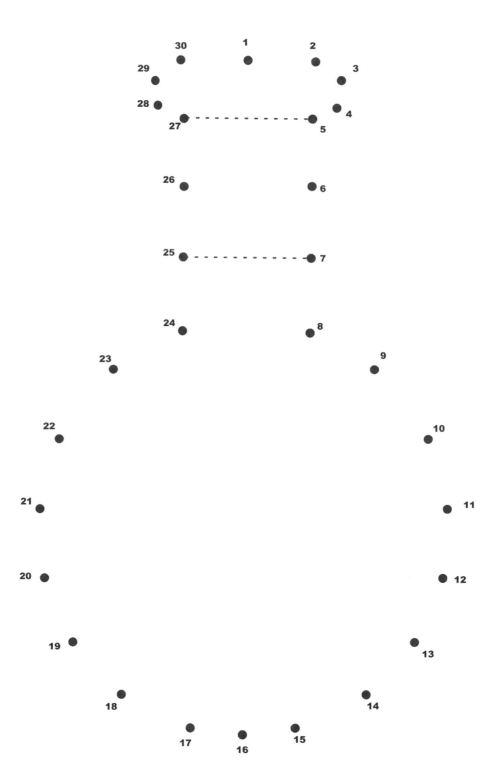

COUNTING NUMBERS

Connect the dots to keep this snow golem from melting.
Count out loud as you go!

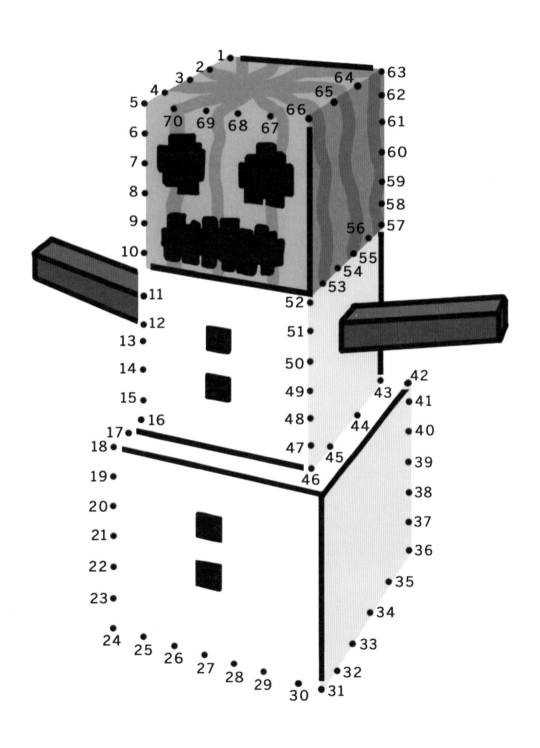

NUMBERS TO 100

Help the villager count the blocks. Fill in the missing numbers.

1	2	3		5	6	7		9	10
11	12		14	15	16		18	19	20
	22	23			26	27	28	29	
31		33	34	35		37	38	39	40
41	42	43		45	46		48		50
51	52		54	55		57		59	
	62	63		65	66		68	69	
71	72		74			77		79	80
		83	84		86	87	88		90
91	92	93		95	96		98	99	100

COUNT BY TWO

The mushrooms in the forest are growing by twos.
Help the witch count the mushrooms.

_____

_____

_____

_____

_____

_____

_____

_____

COUNT BY FIVE

The creepers are planning a big explosion! They have placed the TNT blocks into stacks of five. Count the stacks to find out how many TNT blocks they plan to blow.

     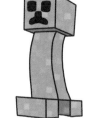

_____ _____ _____

_____ _____ _____ _____ _____

_____ _____ _____ _____

_____ _____ _____ _____ _____

_____ _____ _____ _____

COUNT BY 10

The zombies are coming in groups of 10.
Count by tens to see how many zombies are attacking.

_____   _____   _____

_____   _____   _____

_____   _____   _____

WHAT COMES NEXT?

Look at the pattern. Circle the picture that continues the pattern.

      _____

      _____

      _____

   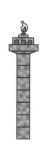   _____

WHAT COMES NEXT?

Look at the pattern. Draw the next picture to continue the pattern.

1.

2.

3.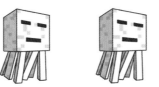

4.

5.

< means less than
> means greater than
= means equal to

COMPARING NUMBERS

Use <, >, or = to compare the numbers.

1. 17 < 19

2. 43 ☐ 34

3. 21 ☐ 26

4. 55 ☐ 55

5. 47 ☐ 74

6. 61 ☐ 51

7. 38 ☐ 37

8. 29 ☐ 30

9. 73 ☐ 63

10. 40 ☐ 50

11. 32 ☐ 81

12. 41 ☐ 41

ADDING

Count and add.

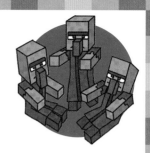

1.

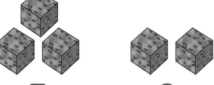

3 + 2 = _____ blocks

2.

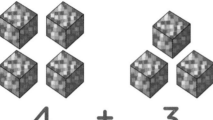

4 + 3 = _____ blocks

3.

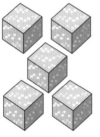

5 + 1 = _____ blocks

4.

2 + 6 = _____ blocks

ADDING

Solve each problem. Draw a line from the equations on each side to the correct answer in the middle. Hint: Each box will have two lines touching it.

8 + 1

2 + 5

3 + 4

4 + 4

2 + 3

3 + 1

2 + 2

5 + 4

1 + 5

1 + 4

6 + 2

3 + 3

ADD WITHIN 10

Solve the problems. Then color each square according to the answer. What Minecrafting object does this look like?

_____

■ 3	■ 4	■ 5	■ 6	■ 7	■ 8	■ 9

2 + 5

6 + 2

9 + 0

3 + 5

7 + 2

2 + 6

7 + 0

6 + 3

7 + 1

5 + 2

3 + 3

2 + 8

8 + 0

4 + 5

2 + 7

3 + 5

6 + 1

2 + 4

4 + 1

2 + 3

3 + 2

5 + 0

3+1

3+0

2+2

1 + 4

4 + 2

3 + 4

1 + 7

6 + 3

5 + 0

1+2

2+1

1+2

5 + 5

1+3

0+3

0+4

0 + 5

2 + 3

4 + 1

8 + 1

4 + 4

0 + 7

5 + 1

4 + 3

7 + 1

5 + 4

5 + 3

1 + 6

5 + 3

7 + 2

2 + 6

1 + 8

0 + 9

63

Add the numbers.
Then compare.

COMPARING NUMBERS

Use <, >, or = to compare the numbers.

1.

3 + 4 ☐ 2 + 5

2.

7 + 2 ☐ 3 + 5

3.

2 + 6 ☐ 6 + 3

4.

1 + 8 ☐ 4 + 5

5.

4 + 2 ☐ 3 + 5

6.

5 + 2 ☐ 2 + 3

7.

1 + 2 ☐ 1 + 1

8.

3 + 3 ☐ 4 + 4

9.

7 + 1 ☐ 5 + 3

10.

4 + 0 ☐ 0 + 5

11.

5 + 2 ☐ 8 + 1

12.

4 + 4 ☐ 5 + 4

MATH ON THE FARM

Read the problem. Draw a picture to solve.

1. Alex collects 6 eggs on Monday and 3 eggs on Tuesday. How many eggs does she collect in all?

   _____

2. Horse ate 2 carrots in the morning. It ate 4 carrots at night. How many carrots did it eat in all? _____

3. There are 3 pigs and 4 baby pigs in the pen. How many pigs are there in all? _____

4. There are 5 sheep in the field and 3 sheep in the barn. How many sheep in all? _____

SUBTRACTING

Read the problem. Cross out to show subtraction.

1. The witch has 6 bottles of potion. The witch splashes 2 bottles. How many bottles of potion are left?

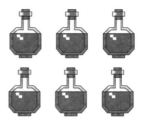

6 - 2 = _____

2. Steve sees 5 bats flying. 4 bats fly away. How many bats are left?

5 - 4 = _____

3. There are 7 spiders. 5 of the spiders are destroyed. How many spiders are left?

7 - 5 = _____

4. The player has 4 firework rockets. The player shoots off 1 firework rocket. How many firework rockets are left?

4 - 1 = _____

SUBTRACTING

Draw a line from the subtraction problem on each side to the correct answer in the middle. Each box will have two lines touching it.

I love to take away!

7 - 5

9 - 3

6 - 1

5 - 1

8 - 7

6 - 3

3 - 2

8 - 3

7 - 1

5 - 2

6 - 4

9 - 5

SUBTRACTING

Solve each problem. Use the answer to solve the riddle.

1. 8 - 6 = _____
A

2. 5 - 4 = _____
E

3. 7 - 3 = _____
L

4. 8 - 3 = _____
T

5. 9 - 2 = _____
B

6. 7 - 1 = _____
D

7. 6 - 3 = _____
H

8. 9 - 1 = _____
S

Question: How did the creeper feel about the dance party?

___ ___ ___ ___ ___ ___ ___ ___ ___ ___ ___ !
3   1   3   2   6   2   7   4   2   8   5

MORE MATH ON THE FARM

Read the problem. Draw a picture to solve.

1. The chickens have 8 eggs, but 3 of them break. How many eggs are left? _____

2. Horse has 6 carrots. It eats 2 carrots. How many carrots are left? _____

3. There are 5 pigs on the farm. 2 become pork chops. How many pigs are left? _____

4. There are 7 rabbits on the farm. Suddenly, 4 rabbits hopped away. How many rabbits are left? _____

MISSING DOTS

Draw the missing dots to add up to the number shown.

6

3

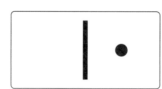

7

5

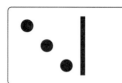

8

4

7

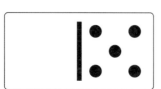

9

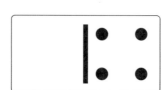

6

WHAT'S MISSING?

Draw the missing hearts to add up to the number on the top of the box. Then write how many hearts you drew.

1.
7	
3	4

♥♥♥

2.
4	
2	

♥♥

3.
8	
4	

♥♥♥♥

4.
9	
6	

♥♥♥
♥♥♥

5.
7	
5	

♥♥♥
♥♥

6.
5	
3	

♥♥♥

7.
6	
4	

♥♥♥♥

8.
8	
5	

♥♥♥
♥♥

9.
9	
2	

♥♥

73

MAKING 10

Color in the blank boxes. Write down how many boxes you colored to finish the addition problem.

1.

$$2 + \boxed{} = \boxed{10}$$

2.

$$5 + \boxed{} = \boxed{10}$$

3.

$$3 + \boxed{} = \boxed{10}$$

4.

$$4 + \boxed{} = \boxed{10}$$

5.

$$7 + \boxed{} = \boxed{10}$$

6.

$$6 + \boxed{} = \boxed{10}$$

MAKING 10

Finish each problem to make 10.

1.

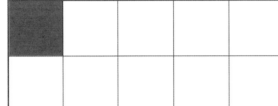

$$1 + \boxed{} = 10$$

2.

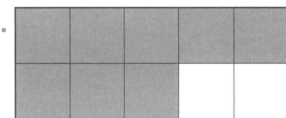

$$8 + \boxed{} = 10$$

3.

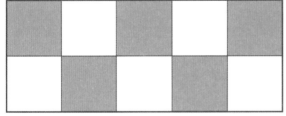

$$5 + \boxed{} = 10$$

4.

$$4 + \boxed{} = 10$$

5.

$$10 + \boxed{} = 10$$

6.

$$0 + \boxed{} = 10$$

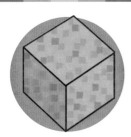

TOWERS OF 10

Count how many blue and red blocks make up each tower of 10.

1.

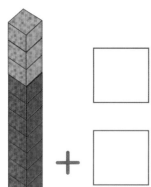 + ☐ ☐

_____

☐10☐ blocks

2.

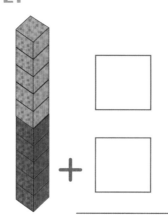 + ☐ ☐

_____

☐10☐ blocks

3.

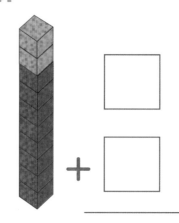 + ☐ ☐

_____

☐10☐ blocks

4.

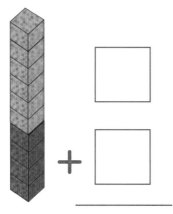 + ☐ ☐

_____

☐10☐ blocks

5.

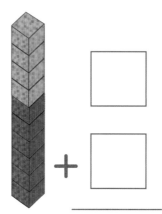 + ☐ ☐

_____

☐10☐ blocks

6.

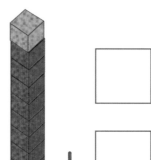 + ☐ ☐

_____

☐10☐ blocks

TOWERS OF 10

Count how many blue and red blocks make up each tower of 10.

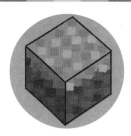

1.

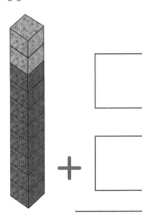 + ☐ ☐ _____ | 10 | blocks

2.

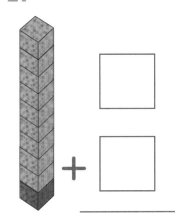 + ☐ ☐ _____ | 10 | blocks

3.

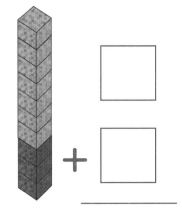 + ☐ ☐ _____ | 10 | blocks

4.

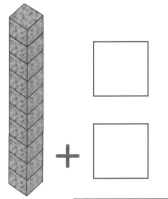 + ☐ ☐ _____ | 10 | blocks

5.

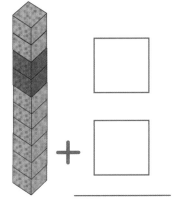 + ☐ ☐ _____ | 10 | blocks

6.

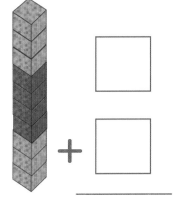 + ☐ ☐ _____ | 10 | blocks

HOW MANY BLOCKS?

Count the towers of 10 and the blocks.

1.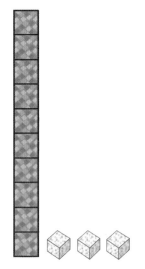

How many? _____

2.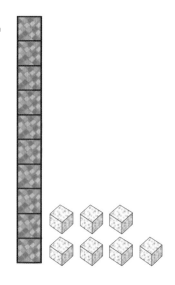

How many? _____

3.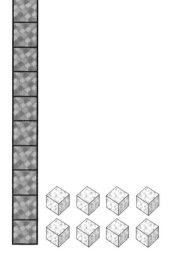

How many? _____

4.

How many? _____

5.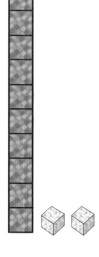

How many? _____

6.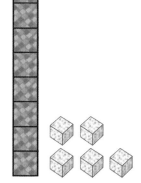

How many? _____

PLACE VALUE

Color the blocks to show how many tens and ones make up each number. The first one is done for you.

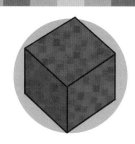

1. **11**

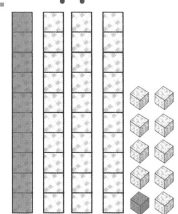

2. **13**

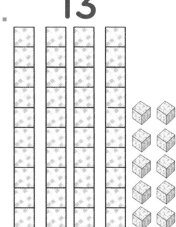

3. **19**

4. **26**

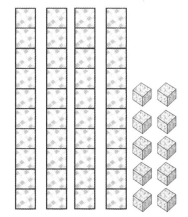

5. **22**

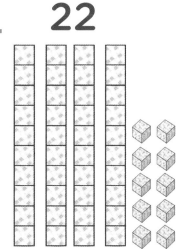

6. **25**

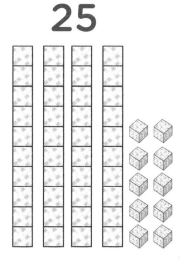

7. **34**

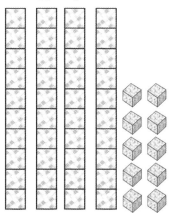

8. **47**

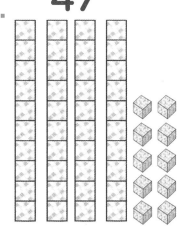

9. **43**

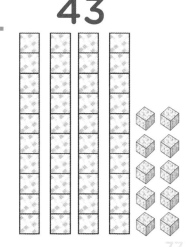

PLACE VALUE

Look at the number. Write how many tens and how many ones.

1.

52	
Tens	Ones

2.

37	
Tens	Ones

3.

24	
Tens	Ones

4.

16	
Tens	Ones

5.

20	
Tens	Ones

6.

41	
Tens	Ones

7.

52	
Tens	Ones

8.

93	
Tens	Ones

9.

75	
Tens	Ones

PLACE VALUE

Look at the number. Write how many tens and how many ones.

1.

82	
Tens	Ones

2.

56	
Tens	Ones

3.

70	
Tens	Ones

4.

61	
Tens	Ones

5.

12	
Tens	Ones

6.

79	
Tens	Ones

7.

95	
Tens	Ones

8.

26	
Tens	Ones

9.

33	
Tens	Ones

Thinking one 10 more in my head makes me feel smart!

TEN MORE

Look at the first number. Add ten in your head. Write the new number.

1. | 20 | 30 |

2. | 50 | |

3. | 30 | |

4. | 44 | |

5. | 62 | |

6. | 71 | |

7. | 15 | |

8. | 36 | |

TEN MORE

Look at the first number. Add ten in your head. Write the new number.

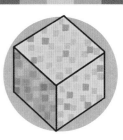

1. | 30 | 40 |

2. | 60 | |

3. | 50 | |

4. | 43 | |

5. | 72 | |

6. | 16 | |

7. | 27 | |

8. | 81 | |

FACT FAMILIES

Look at the fact families. Then fill in the missing numbers.

1.

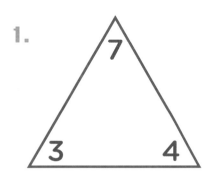

3 + 4 = _____

4 + _____ = 7

7 – 3 = _____

7 – 4 = _____

2.

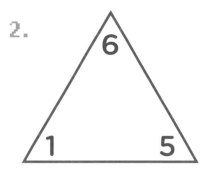

5 + _____ = 6

1 + 5 = _____

6 – 1 = _____

6 – _____ = 1

3.

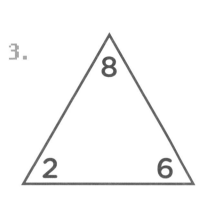

_____ + 6 = 8

2 + 6 = _____

8 – 2 = _____

_____ – 6 = 2

4.

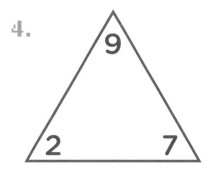

7 + 2 = _____

2 + _____ = 9

9 – 7 = _____

9 – 2 = _____

ADDITION AND SUBTRACTION

Use what is known to solve the unknown.

1. I know **3 + 8 = 11,**
so I know . . .

8 + 3 = _____

11 – 3 = _____

11 – 8 = _____

2. I know **4 + 5 = 9,**
so I know . . .

5 + 4 = _____

9 – 4 = _____

9 – 5 = _____

3. I know **6 + 7 = 13,**
so I know . . .

7 + 6 = _____

13 – 6 = _____

13 – 7 = _____

4. I know **8 + 4 = 12,**
so I know . . .

4 + 8 = _____

12 – 8 = _____

12 – 4 = _____

SHAPES

Trace each shape. Draw your own in the boxes below.

triangle   **square**   **rectangle**   **trapezoid**

1.

2.

triangle

square

3.

4.

rectangle

trapezoid

ZOMBIE INVASION

There is about to be a zombie invasion! Find and circle 1 square and make a check mark inside 6 rectangles in this picture.

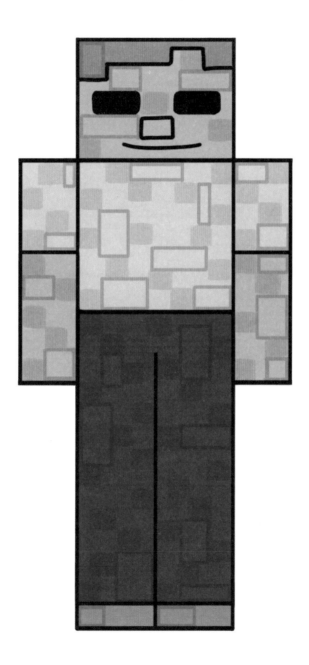

JUST FOR FUN

Question: What did the zombie say when he met a villager?

Answer: So nice to eat you.

Squares look the same upside down!

SHAPE UP!

Follow the directions to help Steve learn about shapes

1. Color the squares red.
2. Color the rectangles blue.
3. Color the triangles green.
4. Color the circles yellow.

SHAPE SHIFTER

Look at each shape. Then complete the chart.

Shape	How Many Sides?	How Many Corners?
triangle		
rhombus		
rectangle		
circle		
square		
hexagon		

TELLING TIME

Look at the clocks. Write the time.

1.

_____ : _____

2.

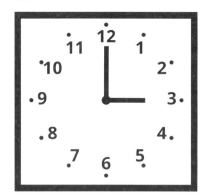

_____ : _____

3.

_____ : _____

4.

_____ : _____

5.

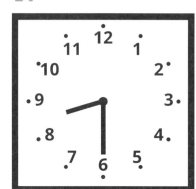

_____ : _____

6.

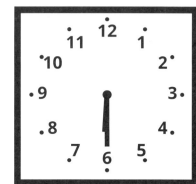

_____ : _____

TELLING TIME

Look at the time. Draw the hands on the clock.

1:00

4:00

11:30

3:00

5:30

10:30

PUSH OR PULL

Look at the pictures. Circle push or pull.

1.

push   pull

2.

push   pull

3.

push   pull

4.

push   pull

PUSH OR PULL

Look at the pictures. Think about how each weapon is used. Circle push or pull. Draw two items in the boxes. One should be something you push. The other should be something you pull.

1.

push   **pull**

2.

push   **pull**

3.

push   **pull**

4.

push   **pull**

Gravity pulls me down!

FORCES IN NATURE

Some forces in nature cause movement. Draw a line to match the force to what it does.

makes windmills turn

WIND

moves dirt and rocks to form canyons

moves a surfer to land

WATER

makes kites fly

make things stick together

MAGNETS

pull things together

GRAVITY

makes things fall to the ground

keeps us on the ground

SCIENCE OPPOSITES

Draw a line connecting the opposites.

Some say I'm the opposite of nice.

1. push

A. backward

2. up

B. pull

3. forward

C. unbalanced

4. throw

D. down

5. balanced

E. catch

93

WEATHER WEAR

Help Alex decide what to wear. Draw a line from each item of clothing to the weather it would be worn in.

WEATHER WORDS

Draw a line to match each weather word to its picture.

1. sun

A.

2. wind

B.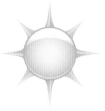

3. cloud

C.

4. rain

D.

5. snow

E.

WEATHER ACTIVITIES

Draw a picture of things you like to do in each kind of weather.

1.

 sunshine

2.

 rain

3.

 snow

4.

 wind

WEATHER FORECAST

Study the forecast. Then answer the questions.

TUE	WED	THU	FRI	SAT	SUN	MON

1. Skeletons and zombies burn up in the sunlight. Which three

days are most dangerous for them? _____

_____

_____

2. Blazes who make it to the Overworld are damaged by rain. On

which days will blazes take damage?_____

_____

3. What is your favorite kind of weather? _____

_____

4. What do you think the weather will be like on Monday? Draw a

picture of your prediction in the forecast box.

MOBS AND ANIMALS

Mobs are living, moving creatures in the Minecrafting world. Some mobs look like animals we see in the real world. Draw a line to connect each mob to its name and matching animal.

1.

chicken

2.

horse

3.

sheep

4.

cow

pig

5.

BABY ANIMALS

Write the name of the animal baby next to each parent.

chick	piglet	calf	lamb	foal

1.   _____

2.   _____

3.  _____

4.   _____

5.   _____

ANIMAL HOMES

Animals have different types of homes. Draw a line to match each animal to its home.

1.

A.

2.

B.

3.

C.

4.

D.

5.

E.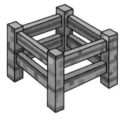

ANIMAL COVERINGS

Just like people wear clothing to protect their bodies, animals have coverings to protect their bodies, too. Draw a line to match each animal to its covering.

I'm softer than I look!

feathers

shell

scales

fur

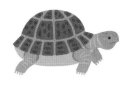

TYPES OF ANIMALS

Read the description of each type of animal. Draw one animal that belongs in each group.

Mammals

Mammals have lungs. They breathe air. They have hair. They give birth to their babies. Baby mammals drink milk. Some mammals are dogs, elephants, whales, and humans.

Reptiles

Reptiles have scales. They lay eggs. They are born on land. They need sun to keep warm. Some reptiles are lizards, snakes, and crocodiles.

Fish

Fish live in water. They have gills, scales, and fins. They breathe through their gills. Some fish are sharks, trout, and goldfish.

Insects

Insects are small animals. They have six legs. They have three body parts. They hatch from eggs. Some insects have wings. Some insects are flies, bees, and grasshoppers.

Amphibians

Amphibians live on both land and water. They lay eggs. They are born in water. They breathe with gills. Some amphibians are frogs and toads.

Birds

Birds have feathers. They have wings. Most birds fly. They lay eggs. Baby birds hatch from eggs. Some birds are owls, robins, and parrots.

WHAT LIVING THINGS NEED

Look at the pictures to see what living things need to survive.
Complete the sentences using one of the words provided.

food   water   shelter   sunlight   air

1. Living things need to eat _____ .

2. _____ shines down and helps plants grow.

3. Humans and animals breathe _____ to live.

4. Homes, nests, and caves are different types of _____ .

5. Living things need to drink _____ .

ANIMAL HABITATS

Just like certain mobs feel more at home in one biome, animals in the real world also have natural homes, or habitats. Draw a line to match each animal to its habitat.

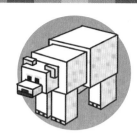

PLANTS

There are many different types of plants. Find the names of these plants and plant-related words in the word find below.

tree	flower	vegetable	fruit	weed
wheat	cactus	bush	vine	grass

```
t  r  i  w  g  r  a  s  s  f
r  t  r  e  e  w  n  u  v  l
f  e  g  e  t  h  a  b  i  o
l  h  s  d  s  e  r  e  n  w
v  e  g  e  t  a  b  l  e  e
b  u  s  h  o  t  r  n  w  r
o  f  r  u  i  t  e  a  t  e
w  e  a  t  c  a  c  t  u  s
```

PARTS OF A PLANT

Label the parts of a plant.

| stem | leaf | petal | roots |

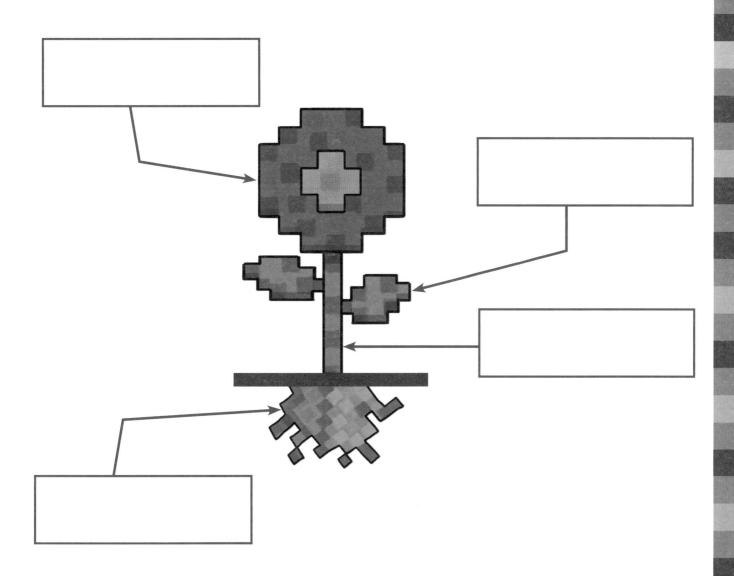

WHAT DO PLANTS NEED TO GROW?

Circle the three things plants need to grow.

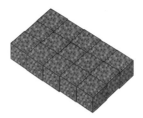

HOW PLANTS GROW

Number the pictures 1 – 6 in the order a plant grows.

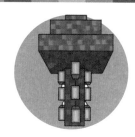

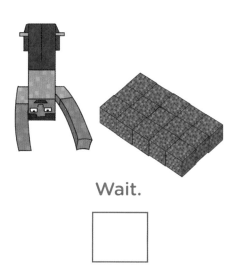

Wait.

Drop a seed in the hole.

Cover the seed with dirt.

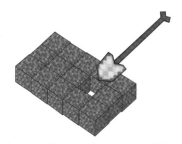

Make a hole in the dirt.

Soon you will have a plant.

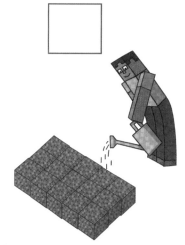

Water the ground.

WATER

Water is everywhere. Write the water words that match each picture.

lake	river	ocean	rain

1.

....

2.

....

3.

....

4.

....

USES OF WATER

Steve uses water to grow food and to keep Endermen away. Check all the ways you have used water today.

Water helps me every day!

☐ to brush my teeth

☐ to wash dishes

☐ to take a bath

☐ to water plants

☐ to wash my hands

☐ to drink

☐ to wash my clothes

☐ to swim

Hey, little villager! You need to eat right to grow big like me.

MY PLATE

When your hunger bar is low, you need to choose healthy foods that give you energy. Look at the foods below. Color the circles next to the fruits red, vegetables green, grains brown, proteins purple, and dairy blue.

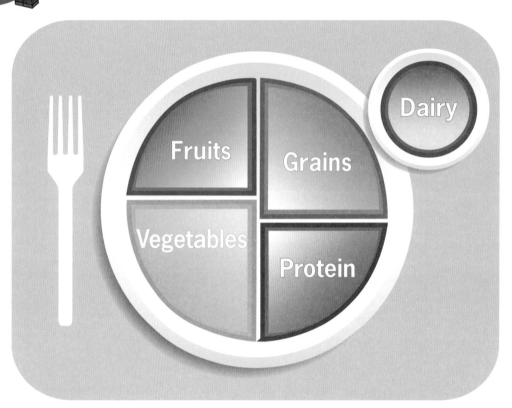

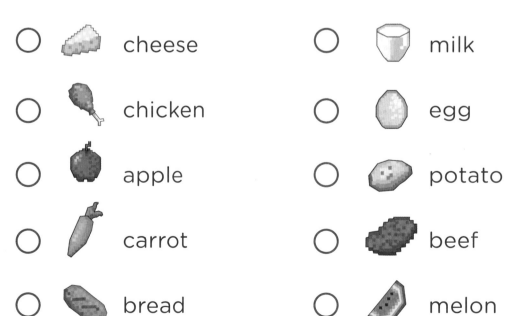

○ cheese

○ chicken

○ apple

○ carrot

○ bread

○ milk

○ egg

○ potato

○ beef

○ melon

HEALTHY FOODS

Complete the crossword.

Nutritious foods give us energy!

| apple | banana | egg | grains |
| milk | meat | nuts | protein |

ACROSS

1 a yellow fruit that needs to be peeled

4 a protein that's hatched

7 meats, eggs, and nuts are part of this food group

8 protein from animals

DOWN

2 a red fruit that's great in pie

3 these are small and tough to crack

5 bread and rice are part of this food group

6 a white dairy drink

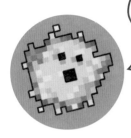

Although not poisonous like me, germs can harm you.

GERMS

Read about germs. Then draw a picture showing how you will keep germs from spreading.

Germs are little creatures. They are so small you can't see them. They are on things you touch, like doorknobs and computer keyboards. They are in the air. To keep germs from spreading, you can:

- wash your hands after you play
- cover your mouth when you sneeze or cough
- use a tissue to blow your nose

HOW I KEEP GERMS FROM SPREADING

STAY HEALTHY

Do you know how to stay healthy? Here are six healthy habits. Use the words in the word box to complete the sentences.

I stay healthy by fighting off hostile mobs!

bath	mouth	teeth	hands	sleep	food

1. Wash your ....

2. Cover your .... when you sneeze.

3. Brush your ....

4. Take a ....

5. Eat nutritious ....

6. Get plenty of ....

PARTS OF THE BODY

Label the parts of the body.

arm	ear	eye	finger	foot	hand
leg	mouth	neck	nose	shoulder	stomach

STEVE VS. THE HUMAN

Label the body parts on Steve. Then compare Steve's body to the human body.

I have   We both have   Steve has

This cake **looks** good and **smells** good. Now, I'll have to see if it tastes good.

OUR FIVE SENSES

Write the sense that matches each body part.

| hear   see   touch   taste   smell |

1. I .... with my eyes.

2. I .... with my nose.

3. I .... with my mouth.

4. I .... with my ears.

5. I .... with my fingers.

BONES IN OUR BODY

Write the names of the parts of a human body.

skull	rib	spine	hand
foot	hip	arm	leg

1.

2.

3.

4.

5.

6.

7.

8.

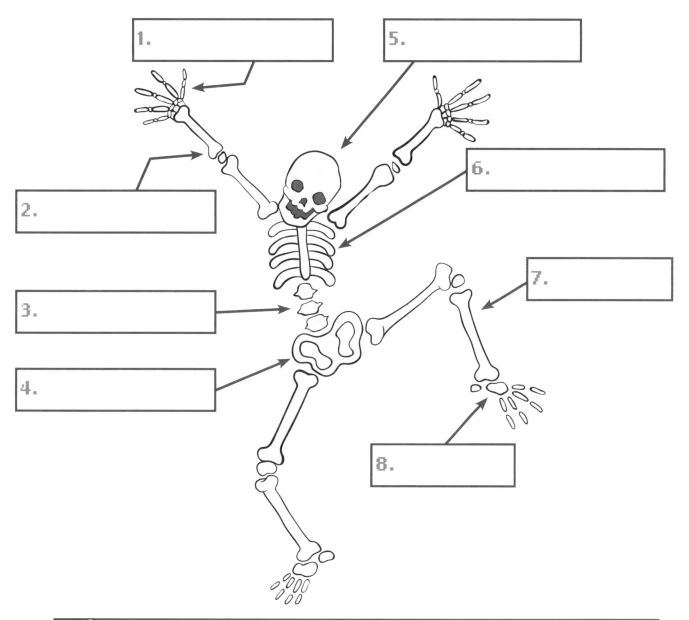

JUST FOR FUN

Question: What instruments do skeletons play?

Answer: The trom-**bone**.

INSIDE MY BODY

Humans are very interesting.

Read about the organs of the body. Then complete the sentences.

Inside your body there are organs that keep you alive. The **lungs** are in the middle of the chest. You have two lungs. They take air in. They also breathe the used air out.

Your **heart** is between your lungs. It moves the blood around your body. The blood carries oxygen and nutrients to every part of the body.

Your **stomach** is below the heart and the lungs. It breaks up the food you eat so your body can use it. From there, food moves to the **small and large intestine.**

Your **organs** work day and night. Even when you're sleeping, your organs are doing their jobs.

1. The .... moves blood around the body.

2. The .... allow you to breathe.

3. The .... breaks up the food you eat.

4. Your .... work even when you are asleep!

INSIDE MY BODY

Label the organs in the body.

I seem to be missing some things.

| heart | small and large intestines |
| lungs | stomach |

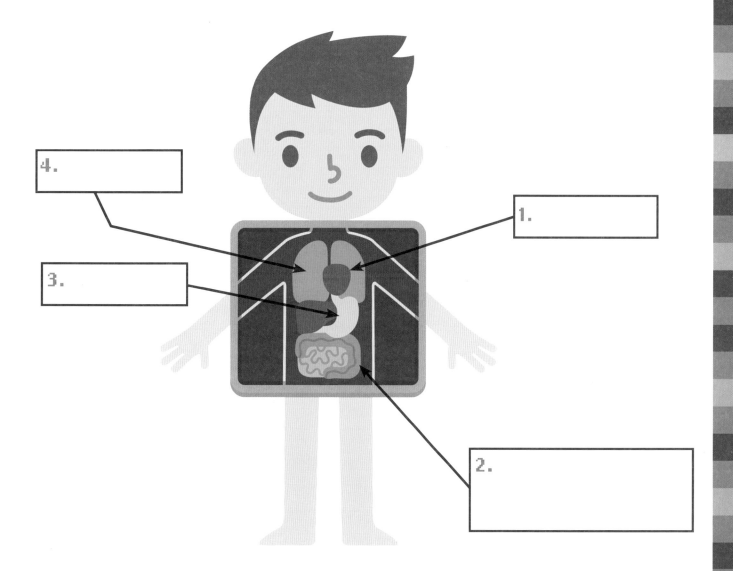

4.

3.

1.

2.

JUST FOR FUN

Question: Why wouldn't the skeleton go sky diving?

Answer: He had no guts!

121

ME AS A PLAYER

Create a player who looks like you. Add hair, eyes, nose, mouth, clothes, and other details. Finish the sentences below.

My hair is ....

My eyes are ....

My skin is ....

My shirt is ....

My pants are ....

WHO AM I?

People and mobs have characteristics. Characteristics are ways to describe a person or thing. Read these characteristics to identify each mob. Draw a picture of each mob.

1.

I am a passive mob that oinks.

I am pink.

I leave pork chops when killed.

2.

I am a hostile mob.

I blow up when you get too close.

I hate cats.

3.

I am a mob you can tame and ride.

I come in many colors.

I am not a donkey or a mule.

4.

I have eight legs.

I climb walls.

I drop string when killed.

WHO AM I?

Make up your own Who Am I? cards describing people or characters you know and see if your friends and family can guess correctly.

HOW'S STEVE FEELING?

Draw a line to match Steve's emotions.

1.

A. angry

2.

B. happy

3.

C. sad

4.

D. scared

5.

E. surprised

EMOTIONS

Write the emotion that describes how each mob is feeling.

sad	embarrassed	proud
bored	angry	happy

1. Horse is _____.
   He tripped and fell in front of everyone.

2.  Witch is _____.
   She has no friends.

3.  Alex is _____.
   She loves being with pig.

4.  Steve is _____.
   He made a wonderful sword.

5. 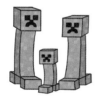 Creepers are _____.
   They lose their temper often!

6. Ghast is _____.
   She has nothing to do.

Even zombie villagers have families.

FAMILIES

Families are made of people. Every family is different. Describe your family. Use the word box if you need help.

mom	stepmom	dad	stepdad
brother	sister		grandma
grandpa	aunt	uncle	cousins

1. I live with _____ __

_____ .

2. I have _____ brothers and _____ sisters.

3. Sometimes I visit _____

_____

_____ .

4. I have _____ aunts and _____ uncles.

5. I have _____ cousins.

MY FAMILY

Draw a picture of your family. Label the picture with the names of the people in your family.

Hanging with our family is a blast.

CELEBRATIONS

Draw a line between each celebration and its matching picture.

1. 4th of July

A.

2. Halloween

B.

3. Birthday

C.

D. ♥♥♥

4. Valentine's Day

E.

5. Thanksgiving

MY FAVORITE CELEBRATION

Write the name of your favorite celebration. Draw a picture of what you do to celebrate.

My favorite celebration is _____.

FRIENDS

Look at what friends do. Then write about what you and your friends like to do.

Friends have fun together.

Friends are kind to each other.

Friends spend time together.

Friends laugh together.

FRIENDS

Check each box that tells something a good friend would do.

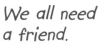

We all need a friend.

☐ **1.** take turns

☐ **2.** share

☐ **3.** push in line

☐ **4.** say something nice

☐ **5.** not let someone play with you

☐ **6.** act rudely

☐ **7.** give a high five

☐ **8.** listen

☐ **9.** tattle

☐ **10.** lie

Needs are things we must have to stay healthy and alive. Wants are things we can live without.

NEEDS AND WANTS

Look at the items. Write **N** for need and **W** for want.

1. house _____

2. candy _____

3. toys _____

4. clothes _____

5. water _____

6. food _____

7. gems _____

NEEDS AND WANTS WORD FIND

Find the needs and wants words in the
word find. Circle one item in red that you need.
Circle one item in orange that you want.

I definitely want to eat this cake.

house	bike	pet	ice cream	ball
food	cookies	bed	water	pool

```
i  c  e  c  r  e  a  m  a  t
c  r  o  o  e  r  i  t  d  p
s  p  o  o  l  h  o  u  s  e
f  o  d  k  r  c  o  e  a  t
o  t  b  i  k  e  l  r  b  k
o  r  a  e  w  a  t  e  r  e
d  n  l  s  e  i  b  e  d  f
e  g  l  o  v  m  i  w  e  a
```

These are strange looking villagers.

JOBS

People get jobs to earn money for the things they need and want.

Write the number of the worker that matches each picture.

1. astronaut

2. judge

3. teacher

4. firefighter

5. journalist

6. police officer

7. chef

8. photographer

....

....

What job do you want when you grow up?

....

....

....

....

GOODS AND SERVICES

Providing a service means you help people do something. A doctor provides a service because he helps us feel better.

I'm a librarian. I provide a service.

Write the service that each worker provides.

1. A doctor ___makes us feel better.___

2. A police officer _____

3. A librarian _____

I'm a farmer. I provide goods.

Providing goods means you create things for people to buy or use. For example, a baker makes bread for us to eat.

Write the good that each worker provides.

1. A baker _____

2. An artist _____

3. A farmer _____

My sword is my tool!

WORKERS AND TOOLS

Match each tool to the worker who uses it.

1. programmer

A.

2. chef

B.

3. artist

C.

4. scientist

D.

5. firefighter

E.

6. doctor

F.

7. judge

G.

PLACES IN MY COMMUNITY

Draw a line to match the words and pictures of places in a community.

1. post office

A.

2. grocery store

B.

3. fire station

C.

4. police station

D.

5. restaurant

E.

6. library

F.

PEOPLE IN MY COMMUNITY

Write the name of each community worker.

| bus driver | firefighter | garbage collector |
| mail carrier | police officer | |

1.

   _____

2.

   _____

3.

   _____

4.

   _____

5.

   _____

HOW I CAN HELP

Good citizens help in their communities. You can be a good citizen. Check the boxes of the things you do to help your community.

☐ Help others.

☐ Don't litter.

☐ Recycle.

☐ Use crosswalks.

☐ Clean up after your pet.

☐ Follow safety rules.

BEING GOOD CITIZENS

*Do you know what it means to be a good citizen? Find out with this quiz. Read each statement. Circle **agree** or **disagree**.*

	agree	disagree
1. Good citizens take pride in their country.	👍	👎
2. Good citizens only help their friends and family.	👍	👎
3. Good citizens respect others.	👍	👎
4. Good citizens criticize others.	👍	👎
5. Good citizens take care of the environment.	👍	👎
6. Good citizens give help to people in need.	👍	👎

Check the answer key to see how you scored on the quiz!

I CAN FOLLOW RULES

Rules are important. Rules allow everyone the same freedoms. Write the rules you follow at home, at school, and in your favorite video game.

Rules at Home

Rules at School

Rules in My Favorite Video Game

THE UNITED STATES

Look at the map of the United States below. Ask an adult to help you answer the questions.

1. How many states are there? _____

2. Place an X on the state where you live.

3. Color the states that you have visited green.

4. Color the states that you want to visit yellow.

MY STATE

Write the name of your state. Draw a picture of it. Include some pictures of things you like about your state.

_____

My State

U.S. SYMBOLS

Color the flag of the United States. Count the stars.

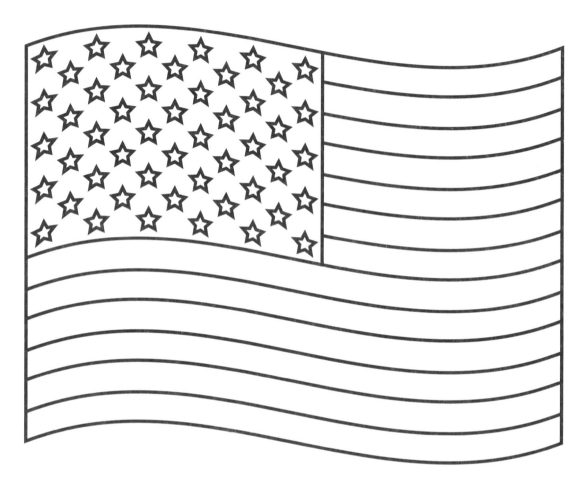

There are _____ stars on the American flag.

Each star is a symbol of

_____.

On a separate piece of paper, design a Minecrafting flag that celebrates what you love most about Minecrafting!

U.S. SYMBOLS

Draw a line to match each U.S. symbol with its name.

America is the home of the brave!

1.

A. White House

2.

B. Bald Eagle

3.

C. American Flag

4.

D. Statue of Liberty

5.

E. Liberty Bell

LANDFORMS

Draw a line from each landform word to its picture.

1. mountain

A.

2. island

B.

3. canyon

C.

4. hill

D.

5. volcano

E.

OCEANS AND CONTINENTS

I've read a lot about Earth. It's a big place!

Look at the map. Then follow the directions to color the map.

We live on Earth. Earth is round. Earth is made up of land and water. Large areas of land are called **continents**. Earth has seven continents. Large areas of water are called **oceans**. Earth has five oceans.

1. Color Africa yellow.

2. Color Antarctica pink.

3. Color Asia orange.

4. Color Australia green.

5. Color Europe purple.

6. Color North America red.

7. Color South America brown.

8. Color all the oceans blue.

RELATIVE LOCATION

Look at the picture. Circle the word that makes each sentence correct.

1. The Enderman is **inside / outside** the haunted house.

2. The zombie is **above / below** the front door.

3. The witch on the broom is **near / far**.

4. The creeper is to the **right / left** of the spider.

5. The Jack o' Lantern is **behind / in front** of the haunted house.

READING A MAP

Read the map of a farm. Answer the questions.

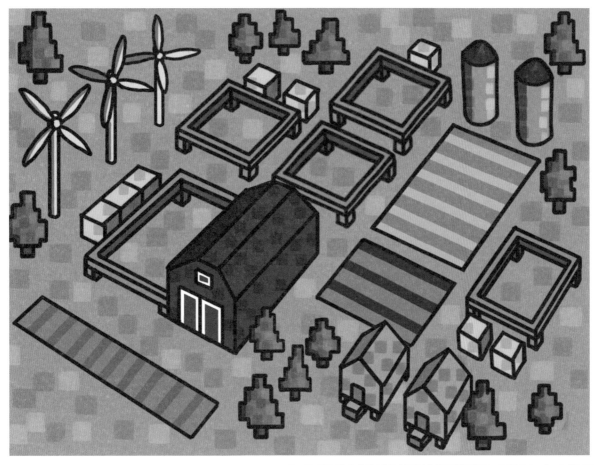

Hay	Pen	Windmill	Barn	Silo	Chicken House	
Crop						

1. How many windmills are there? _____

2. How many bales of hay are there? _____

3. What building is left of the chicken houses? _____

4. Circle where you see crops growing.

5. Draw 2 pigs in one of the pens.

ANSWER KEY

PAGE 6

1. Bb

2. Dd

3. Pp

4. Tt

5. Ss

PAGE 7

1. Cc

2. Ff

3. Mm

4. Rr

5. Ww

PAGE 8
1. C; 2. A; 3. B; 4. E; 5. D

PAGE 9
1. short; 2. long; 3. short; 4. short; 5. short;
6. long; 7. short; 8. short; 9. long

PAGE 10
1. E; 2. C; 3. B; 4. A; 5. D

PAGE 11
1. map; 2. egg; 3. fish; 4. block; 5. web; 6. bat;
7. hug; 8. squid

PAGE 12
1. cake; 2. bone; 3. mule; 4. ride; 5. cube

PAGE 13
1. D; 2. A; 3. E; 4. C; 5. B

PAGE 14
1. He went to the library.
2. He wanted to find a book of enchantment to defeat the Wither.
3. Yes, he did.

PAGE 15
Answers may vary.

PAGE 16
1. Steve walks through the woods.
2. Zombies attack, and Steve and the zombies fight.
3. Steve destroys the zombies.

PAGE 17
1. Steve and his dog must save the farm from the skeletons.
2. Steve and his dog fight against the skeletons.
3. Steve and his dog save the farm.

PAGE 19
1. P - It is near water.
2. W - It is made of clay and glass.
3. W / P - It has tall buildings.
4. W - Villagers and visitors.
5. W / P – You can walk, ride the train, or take a boat.

PAGE 20
1. mean; 2. people who live in a place; 3. to create;
4. places with special plants and land types

PAGE 21
1. neither bad nor good; 2. a swampy forest;
3. empty; 4. dangerous

PAGE 22

1.

2.

3.

4.

5.

PAGE 23

1.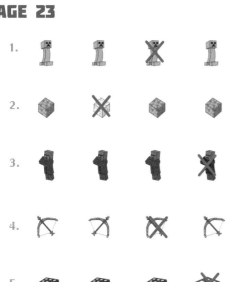

PAGE 24

1. D; 2. C; 3. A; 4. B

PAGE 25

1. living; 2. nonliving; 3. green; 4. red; 5. 4 legs; 6. 2 legs

PAGE 26

Animal: cow
Food: melon
Weapon: golden sword
Plant: flower

PAGE 27

1. by; 2. on; 3. in; 4. above; 5. beside; 6. on

PAGE 28

PAGE 29

1. pigs; 2. potatoes; 3. witches' 4. cows; 5. bushes

PAGE 30

1. fight; 2. swim; 3. eat; 4. laugh; 5. run; 6. ride; 7. fly; 8. think; 9. sit

PAGE 31

1. D; 2. B; 3. E; 4. A; 5. C

PAGE 32

1. The snow golem is a mob. 2. It has two snow blocks and a pumpkin head. 3. It throws snowballs. 4. Does it melt when it gets hot? 5. Does it melt in the rain?

PAGE 33

1. !; 2. .; 3. ?; 4.?; 5. .; 6. .; 7. or !; 8. ! or .

PAGE 34

1. Steve cuts the cake. 2. Dragon flies through blocks. 3. Trees grow in the Overworld. 4. Alex cares for chickens and pigs.

PAGE 35

Answers will vary.

PAGE 36

Answers will vary.

PAGE 37

Answers will vary.

PAGE 38–39

Answers will vary.

PAGE 40–41

Answers will vary.

PAGE 42

1 Use the diamond to make a sword.

2 Put the diamond in the chest.

4 Locate a block of diamond ore.

3 Use an iron pickaxe to break the block.

PAGE 43

2 Put the saddle on the pig.

1 You will need a pig, a saddle, a carrot, and a stick.

4 Jump on the pig.

3 Hook the carrot on the stick and hold it out.

PAGE 44

Answers will vary.

PAGE 45

Answers will vary.

PAGE 46

Answers will vary.

PAGE 47

Answers will vary.

PAGE 48

creeper   zombie pigman

PAGE 49

1. 4; 2. 9; 3. 6; 4. 1; 5. 3 ; 6. 8; 7. 2; 8. 5; 9. 4

PAGE 50

9 animals; 28 legs

PAGE 51

1 shark; 20 blue fish; 1 purple fish; 1 squid;
3 orange fish; 1 pink fish; 1 crab

PAGE 52

potion bottle

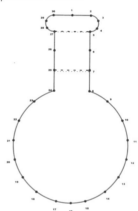

PAGE 53

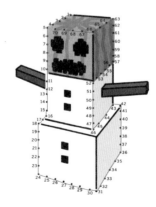

PAGE 54

4, 8, 13, 17, 21, 24, 25, 30, 32, 36, 44, 47, 49, 53, 56, 58,
60, 61, 64, 67, 70, 73, 75, 76, 78, 81, 82, 85, 89, 94, 97

PAGE 55

2, 4, 6, 8, 10, 12, 14, 16

PAGE 56

5, 10, 15, 20, 25, 30, 35, 40, 45, 50, 55, 60, 65, 70, 75, 80, 85, 90, 95, 100, 105

PAGE 57

10, 20, 30, 40, 50, 60, 70, 80, 90

PAGE 58

PAGE 59

PAGE 60

1. <; 2. >; 3. <; 4. =; 5. <; 6. >; 7. >; 8. <; 9. >; 10. <; 11. <; 12 =

PAGE 61

1. 5 blocks; 2. 7 blocks; 3. 6 blocks; 4. 8 blocks

PAGE 62

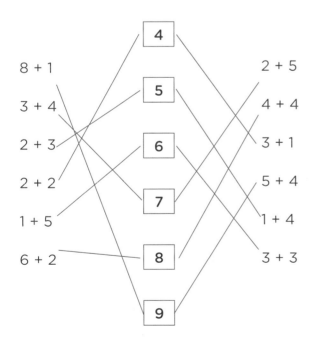

PAGE 63

It's an experience orb!

PAGE 64

1. =; 2. >; 3. <; 4. =; 5. <; 6. >; 7. >; 8. <; 9. =; 10. <; 11. <; 12. <

PAGE 65

1. 9 eggs; 2. 6 eggs; 3. 7 pigs; 4. 8 sheep

PAGE 66

1. 4; 2. 1; 3. 2; 4. 3

PAGE 67

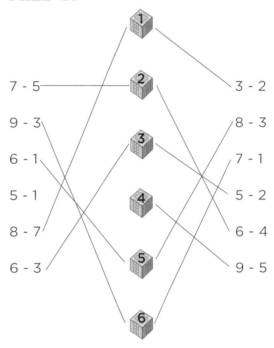

PAGE 68

1. 2; 2. 1; 3. 4; 4. 5; 5. 7; 6; 7. 3; 8. 8
He had a blast!

PAGE 69

1. 5; 2. 4; 3. 3; 4. 3

PAGE 70

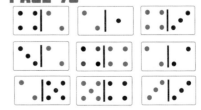

PAGE 71

1. 4; 2. 2; 3. 4; 4. 3; 5. 2; 6. 2; 7. 2; 8. 3; 9. 7

PAGE 72

1. 8; 2. 5; 3. 7; 4. 6; 5. 3; 6. 4

PAGE 73

1. 9
2. 2
3. 5
4. 6
5. 0
6. 10

PAGE 74

1. 3 blue, 7 red; 2. 5 blue, 5 red; 3. 8 blue, 2 red;
4. 6 blue, 4 red; 5. 4 blue, 6 red; 6. 1 blue, 9 red

PAGE 75

1. 2 blue, 8 red; 2. 9 blue, 1 red; 3. 7 blue, 3 red;
4. 10 blue, 0 red; 5. 8 blue, 2 red; 6. 6 blue, 4 red

PAGE 76

1. 13; 2. 17; 3. 18; 4. 14; 5. 12; 6. 15

PAGE 77

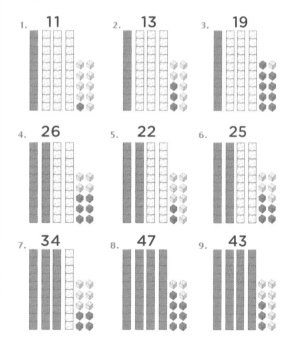

PAGE 78

1. 52		2. 37		3. 24	
Tens	Ones	Tens	Ones	Tens	Ones
5	2	3	7	2	4

4. 16		5. 20		6. 41	
Tens	Ones	Tens	Ones	Tens	Ones
1	6	2	0	4	1

7. 52		8. 93		9. 75	
Tens	Ones	Tens	Ones	Tens	Ones
5	2	9	3	7	5

PAGE 79

1. 82		2. 56		3. 70	
Tens	Ones	Tens	Ones	Tens	Ones
8	2	5	6	7	0

4. 61		5. 12		6. 79	
Tens	Ones	Tens	Ones	Tens	Ones
6	1	1	2	7	9

7. 95		8. 26		9. 33	
Tens	Ones	Tens	Ones	Tens	Ones
9	5	2	6	3	3

PAGE 80

1. 30; 2. 60; 3. 40; 4. 54; 5. 72; 6. 81; 7. 25; 8. 46

PAGE 81

1. 20; 2. 50; 3. 40; 4. 33; 5. 62; 6. 6; 7. 17; 8. 71

PAGE 82

1. 3 + 4 = 7; 4 + 3 = 7 ; 7 – 3 = 4; 7 – 4 = 3
2. 5 + 1 = 6; 1 + 5 = 6; 6 – 1 = 5; 6 – 5 = 1
3. 2 + 6 = 8; 2 + 6 = 8; 8 – 2 = 6; 8 - 6 = 2
4. 7 + 2 = 5; 2 + 7 = 9 ; 9 – 7 = 2 ; 9 – 2 = 7

PAGE 83

1. 8 + 3 = 11; 11 – 3 = 8 ; 11 – 8 = 3
2. 5 + 4 = 9; 9 – 4 = 5 ; 9 – 5 = 4
3. 7 + 6 = 13; 13 – 6 = 7 ; 13 – 7 = 6
4. 4 + 8 = 12; 12 – 8 = 4 ; 12 – 4 = 8

PAGE 84

Answers will vary.

PAGE 85

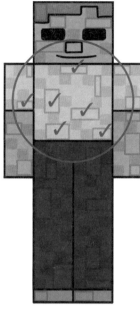

PAGE 86

PAGE 87

Shape	How Many Sides?	How Many Corners?
triangle	3	3
rhombus	4	4
rectangle	4	4
circle	0	0
square	4	4
hexagon	6	6

PAGE 88

1. 10:00; 2. 3:00; 3. 7:00; 4. 2:30; 5. 8:30; 6. 6:30

PAGE 89

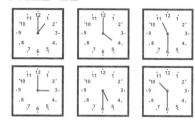

PAGE 90

1. pull; 2. pull; 3. pull; 4. push

PAGE 91

1. pull; 2. push

PAGE 92

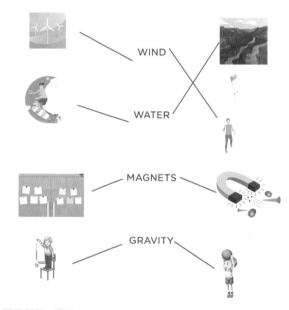

PAGE 93

1. B; 2. D; 3. A; 4. E; 5. C

PAGE 94

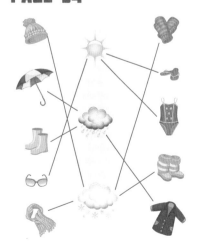

PAGE 95

1. B; 2. C; 3. E; 4. D; 5. A

PAGE 96

Answer will vary.

PAGE 97

1. Thursday, Friday, Sunday 2. Tuesday, Wednesday 3. Answer will vary. 4. Answer will vary.

PAGE 98

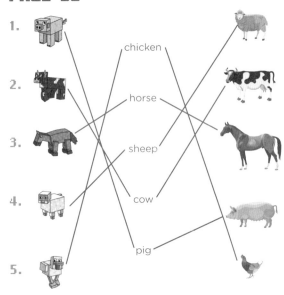

PAGE 99

1. lamb; 2. calf; 3. foal; 4. chick; 5. piglet

PAGE 100

1. B; 2. A; 3. D; 4. E; 5. C

PAGE 101—

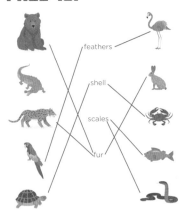

PAGE 102, 103

Answers will vary.

PAGE 104

1. food; 2. sunlight; 3. air; 4. shelter; 5. water

PAGE 105

PAGE 106

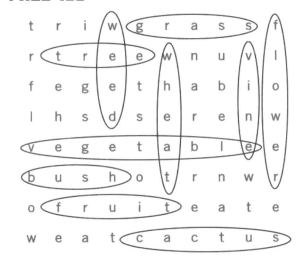

PAGE 107

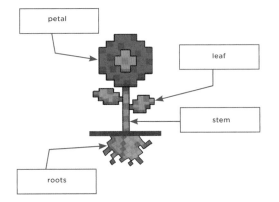

156

PAGE 108

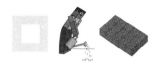

PAGE 109

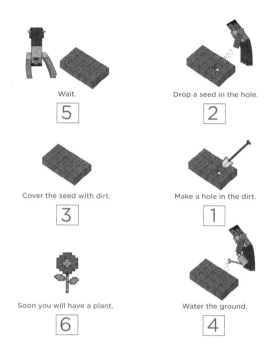

Wait.
5

Drop a seed in the hole.
2

Cover the seed with dirt.
3

Make a hole in the dirt.
1

Soon you will have a plant.
6

Water the ground.
4

PAGE 110

1. rain; 2. lake; 3. ocean; 4. river

PAGE 111

Answers will vary.

PAGE 112

- cheese
- chicken
- apple
- carrot
- bread
- milk
- egg
- potato
- beef
- melon

PAGE 113

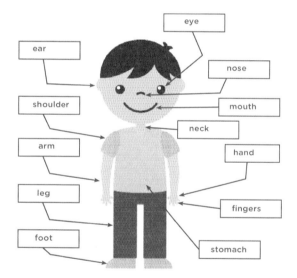

PAGE 114

Answers will vary.

PAGE 115

1. hands; 2. mouth; 3. teeth; 4. bath; 5. food;
6. sleep

PAGE 116

PAGE 117

157

PAGE 118
1. see; 2. smell; 3. taste; 4. hear; 5. touch

PAGE 119
1. hand; 2. arm; 3. spine; 4. hip; 5. skull; 6. rib; 7. leg; 8. foot

PAGE 120
1. heart; 2. lungs; 3. stomach; 4. organs

PAGE 121
1. heart; 2. large and small intestines; 3. stomach; 4. lungs

PAGE 122
Answers will vary.

PAGE 123
1. pig; 2. creeper; 3. horse; 4. spider

PAGE 124
1. C; 2. E; 3. A; 4. B; 5. D

PAGE 125
1. hungry; 2. sad; 3. happy; 4. proud; 5. angry;
6. bored; 7. scared; 8. excited; 9. confused

PAGE 126, 127
Answers will vary.

PAGE 128
1. E; 2. A; 3. C; 4. D; 5. B

PAGE 129, 130
Answers will vary.

PAGE 131
Boxes 1, 2, 4, 7, 8, should be checked.

PAGE 132
1. N; 2. W; 3. W; 4. N; 5 N; 6. N; 7. W

PAGE 133
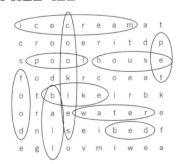

PAGE 134
4, 7, 3, 1, 2, 5, 6, 8

PAGE 135
Answers will vary.

PAGE 136
1. E; 2. C; 3. D; 4. G; 5. F; 6. A; 7. B

PAGE 137
1. C 2. E 3. D 4. B 5. F 6. A

PAGE 138
1. mail carrier; 2. fire fighter; 3. police officer;
4. garbage collector; 5. bus driver

PAGE 139
Answers will vary.

PAGE 140
1. agree; 2. disagree; 3. agree; 4. disagree;
5. agree; 6. agree

PAGES 141
Answers will vary.

PAGES 142
1. 50 states

PAGES 143–144
Answers will vary.

PAGE 145
1. D; 2. B; 3. A; 4. E; 5. C

PAGE 146
1. C; 2. D; 3. B; 4. E; 5. A

PAGE 147

PAGE 148
1. inside; 2. above; 3. far; 4. right; 5. in front

PAGE 149
1. 3; 2. 8; 3. barn